The Isle of Skye

Text by Jim Crumley

Photography by Colin Baxter

Colin Baxter Photography Ltd, Grantown-on-Spey, Scotland

There is no hill range of Scotland which varies so greatly in aspect as the Cuillin of Skye. With the weather their mood changes suddenly. They smile or are sad; they frown and are terrible.

Seton Gordon, *The Charm of Skye*

Sgurr Alasdair, chieftain of the Cuillin, and its Pinnacle Ridge. The mountain was first climbed in 1873.

IT SHOULD BEGIN with the Cuillin. The Island of Skye wears that singular mountainous flourish the way a chief in the long-lost heyday of the clans would wear eagle feathers in his cap, a badge of pre-eminence. Skye is the chief of Scotland's clan of islands, the Cuillin the eagle feathers in its cap.

If you are extraordinarily lucky, your very first view of the Cuillin will be on a blue day in May and from Arisaig *en route* from Fort William to Mallaig and the Skye ferry. On such a day and from such a distance the seagoing profile of the Cuillin is among the most unlikely things on earth. A gold band of light lies along the hem of its skirts, a flamboyant stitching. Your eyes tell you the mountains have lifted bodily up out of both land and sea, your head tells you such things are the fruits of hallucination. Both are right. The sea mirage is a phenomenon of the light's clarity, of a clear northern air. The Inuit of Arctic Canada have a word for it that translates as 'up in the air'.

It is an invaluable first insight with which to greet the island, for there is much an exploration of the Skye landscape reveals

The unforgettable view of the Cuillin from Elgol on the shore of Loch Scavaig.

The Cuillin in winter. 'They rise like the hills of a land of dreams.' Here seen from the north-west across Loch Bracadale.

but does not explain. You will live easier with that truth if you have seen for yourself at the outset that the Cuillin can float. Already you see that analogy with eagle feathers is no idle fancy.

The Cuillin have their own chieftain:

'No man could wish for a memorial more lasting or more wonderful than the dark, wind-swept pinnacle of Sgurr Alasdair. The peak is named after the late Sheriff Alasdair Nicolson, a son of Skye, poet and writer, who, in 1873, first climbed to a summit that was hitherto considered inaccessible.

'Sgurr Alasdair and its attendant peaks, seen from some outpost of the range on a winter's day, are memorable. The eye rests upon white spires, cones, and pinnacles. They rise like the hills of a land of dreams. Upon them is a wild and lonely beauty

– a beauty that transports the spirit of him who sees it beyond the realm of time and space to a spiritual land of beauty, wonder, and mystery.'

The writer was Seton Gordon, who lived for much of his adult life at Duntulm in the north of Skye, and whose book, *The Charm of Skye*, written in 1929, is itself no meagre memorial, a pinnacle in the literature of the island. See how he treads that fine line between what is seen and what is sensed. On Skye of all places, that double vision is all-pervasive.

The Black Cuillin, the profile you saw floating off Arisaig, are made of gabbro, a razor-edged rock that can shred a pair of climbing boots in a season or a pair of unaccustomed hands in an afternoon, but it is wondrously adhesive stuff for climbing on. That quality of the rock, the barely credible beauty of the range, the rarified ridge-and-pinnacle summits, the limitless views of island and ocean, the sense of participating in the very history

The horseshoe-shaped main ridge of the Cuillin, with Loch Coruisk at its heart.

The Cuillin outpost of Sgurr na Stri guards the entrance to Loch Coruisk. The short sea crossing from Elgol is one of Skye's most memorable excursions.

of mountaineering (for it was in the Cuillin that some of the greatest pioneers came of age)...all these set the Cuillin apart as a mountaineering theatre.

But non-climbers are drawn too, to walk in the mountains' shadows, or merely to marvel. Even in the heady company of all the mountains of Scotland's western seaboard, the Cuillin stand alone, without equal, beyond trite comparison. That *bodach* of mountain photography, W.A. Poucher, called them 'nature's masterpiece in the Highlands'.

He would know. He photographed them for 50 years.

And Seton Gordon offered them this thoughtful tribute:

'There is no hill range of Scotland which varies so greatly in aspect...With the weather their mood changes suddenly. They smile or are sad; they frown and are terrible. The dun wind from the Atlantic reaches their blue, clear-cut spires, and immediately a mist curtain is drawn across them; before the coming of a storm they clothe themselves with the blue mantle of mystery.

'Then there are days when the Cuillin are alive with benign spiritual forces; when the hill silence tells of many wonderful things; when hill, sky, and ocean glow with life and energy.'

The same tribute is no less appropriate to the island itself.

Skye is a big island by Hebridean standards, 60 miles from north to south and none of them short miles. Devising a satisfactory east-west measurement is more difficult, for the landmass is assailed by long sea lochs from every compass point. You could draw a straight line from the island capital, Portree, on the east coast, to Neist Point on the west, and pronounce the island 25 miles wide, but at no point on such a line would you find yourself more than four miles from the sea. Another straight line from Portree to the northwest would reach Skye's western seaboard at Loch Snizort Beag in only six miles.

Bla Beinn, seen here across Loch Slapin, is a mountain superstar by any standards, and arguably the most beautiful not just on Skye but in all Scotland.

These sea lochs create the character of Skye, carve the landscape into 'wings', and caused men to christen the place Eilean Sgiathanach, the Winged Island. And the Vikings, whose legacy is everywhere in the place names of Skye, called it *Skuyo*, Island of Cloud, which has in turn been Gaelicised as Eilean a' Cheo, and Anglicised as the Misty Isle, a phrase beloved of bad songs and a now more or less defunct strain of hopelessly romantic tourism. Nevertheless, Skye is not short of mist, cloud, or wings, and the natives are inclined to call it simply The Island, and as such it is remembered by exiles all across the world.

You will find quite a number of people who love it in a way shared by no other island of the west coast: people who understand, or are ready to understand, the meaning of the famous saying that Skye is not an island but an intoxication.

Sir William Tarn in his Foreword to Otta Swire's *Skye, the Island and its Legends*.

Point of Sleat is the southmost tip of Skye's southmost peninsula. On the seaward horizon lie two of the characteristic shapes of the Small Isles – low-slung Eigg and mountainous Rum.

If you board the island from Mallaig, your landfall is Armadale on the Sleat peninsula (you must say 'Slate' and not the fatal 'Sleet') among trees and a certain lushness. It is a deception, enhanced by the famous gardens around Armadale Castle, an old MacDonald eminence, and more or less all the way up the ribbon of road that clings to Sleat's east coast. On the strength of that greenery Sleat claims for itself the less-than-honest title of the Garden of Skye. But Armadale and the roadside trees apart, there is precious little garden on Sleat.

Take the little hill road across to the west coast of Sleat, to Tarskavaig and Ord, and enter a wild world of high moor, rock outcrop, crag and lochan, that characterises much of inland Skye. From the watershed there are oceanic sightlines to islands beyond and the sudden and astounding proximity of the Cuillin. It is this aspect of Sleat, not its 'garden', that hallmarks it as quintessential Skye. Other islands are forever cropping up, and the Cuillin's capacity to astound by appearing like a rabbit out of a hat is a trick of Skye that never palls, and no corner of the island is immune to it.

On Sleat, too, if you have the luck and the patience and the eyes, you may see golden eagles, white-tailed eagles, otters, divers, whooper swans, hen harriers and deer, and all these are characteristic wildlife tribes of Skye. It is yet

The Cuillin from Sleat. 'There are days when they are alive with benign spiritual forces; when the hill silence tells of many wonderful things; when hill, sky and ocean glow with life and energy…'.

another trait of the island that you are likely to be confronted by everything at once, and either overwhelmed by it all or addicted forever.

Sir William Tarn, writing in a foreword to Otta Swire's popular and enduring book, *Skye, The Island and its Legends*, included this sentiment:

'…you will find quite a number of people who love it in a way shared by no other island of the west coast: people who understand, or are ready to understand, the meaning of the famous saying that Skye is not an island but an intoxication. That is a matter of *feeling*, which can no more be explained in cold print than any other form of love; but some of us know very well that it exists. It is the *spirit* of the island, of the land itself, and of the people who have made it…'

It is remarkable how many different writers are willing to

The rounded sandstone shapes of the Red Hills dominate the view west across Broadford Bay, with Beinn na Caillich – last resting place of a Norse princess – for their centrepiece.

accord Skye an element of the spiritual, the unseen, the landscape of the mind. Painters too, witness Turner's account of Loch Coruisk at the heart of the Cuillin, a painting that reaches for something more than a configuration of rock and light and water. If you are new to Skye, it is worth knowing about the dangers of the intoxication, not that you are likely to be able to do much about it, or want to for that matter.

The oldest crossing to Skye is also the shortest, the least used, the most beautiful by far. A giddy little road heaves and swerves west from Shiel Bridge, up over Mam Rattagan and down through Glen More to Glenelg Bay, where a tiny ferry slips across the quarter-of-a-mile-wide Sound to Kylerhea, a road-end with a pier, an otter-watching hide and not much else. The narrowness of the crossing was its historical virtue, but if you watch the tide barge through Kyle Rhea into the Sound of Sleat, and remind yourself that islanders used to swim their cattle to the mainland here, you suppress a shudder and wait, patiently and gratefully, for the wee ferry to trundle back. Glen Arroch, another heaving, swerving little road, lies beyond Kylerhea, as empty and wild a corner of Skye as you will find, a troubling first encounter if that is what you have chosen.

Kyle of Lochalsh is the principal gateway, and now that the last ferry has sailed from its pier and Skye is bridged to the mainland like a peninsula, crossing over has never been easier, and is now free since the tolls were scrapped at the end of 2004. You can also walk across, and whether you find the concrete bridge loathsome or lovable, the view from the top of its steep arch is as spectacular as it is airy, and with novelty to recommend it too.

One consequence of the bridge is that the old ferry landfall of Kyleakin has been by-passed. In time, though, it may well grow into a base for a more thoughtful kind of visitor than the on-off press of ferry traffic ever permitted. The walk round to Castle Maol reveals a hidden charm and there is just enough dicing with incoming tides about the castle's footpath to spice the walk. The castle is a 12th-century fragment. Perch among 11 ft-thick walls, ruminate on the legend surrounding a Norwegian Princess with the unlikely name of Saucy Mary (doubtless something has been lost, or added, in the translation). The castle, recently stabilised and floodlit, invites you to contemplate a time when the Sound and all its shipping could be commanded from this one rock. It remains among Skye's most alluring stone souvenirs.

Broadford is as unavoidable as Kyleakin is sidelined, a long village strung out by townships round a wide and lovely bay, and with far views of mainland mountains. It is also in thrall to Beinn

The controversial Skye Bridge which replaced the car ferry between Kyleakin (right) and Kyle of Lochalsh on the Scottish mainland in 1995. Eilean Ban beneath the bridge was the last home of the writer Gavin Maxwell.

na Caillich, a huge bitten curve of a hill topped with an outrageously large cairn, the last resting place, so it is said, of the same Saucy Mary. The labour such a cairn – and such a burial – would have entailed suggests a revered corpse, whether saucy or otherwise.

Beinn na Caillich also introduces the traveller to the Red Cuillin, a range of hills joined at the hip to the Black Cuillin by way of a geological hinge. You see it best from the road above Luib on the way north, and the chalk-and-cheese relationship of Red and Black is massively and unforgettably unfurled at Sligachan.

The Red Cuillin are smooth shapes, slabs and curves and angles of Torridonian sandstone liberally showered with pink screes, and as unlike the Black Cuillin as any mountains anywhere.

Evening sun puts deep Burgundy shades among the Red Cuillin, a shade much admired along the first half of the single track road between Broadford and Elgol, another of those east-west coast-to-coast roads that repay close scrutiny. This one also boasts two of Skye's great set pieces: the massive side-on profile of Bla Bheinn (a robustly individualistic outlier of the Black Cuillin), and the view of the Cuillin from Elgol itself. With added sunset, that view is a Skye cliché, albeit a cliché which can last you a lifetime if you encounter it on the right kind of evening. All who suffer the Skye intoxication have their Elgol-at-sunset stories to tell.

The Broadford-Elgol road is also the starting point for a

An eagle's eye-view of Bla Bheinn, looking south.

The Red Hills, looking southeast over Glas Bheinn Mhor to Beinn na Caillich, with Loch na Sguabaidh to the right.

Boreraig, Loch Eishort, one of the most infamous names in the narrative of the Highland Clearances.

Marsco, the most handsome mountain in the Red Cuillin, towers above Glen Sligachan, a familiar sight to all who pause at the Sligachan Hotel.

journey on foot into the island's uncomfortable past, footpaths to Boreraig and Suisnish, grim chapters both in the narrative of the Highland Clearances. Both are singularly affecting places, in which the beauty of the landscape mocks the roofless ruins and the aura of despair which prevails still.

North of Broadford the main road tiptoes eastabout between the foot of the Red Cuillin and the sea. The whole mass of the Cuillin is a slung barrier right across the island waist which all Skye's travellers have had to negotiate. There are footpaths through the hills, but these make for arduous treks in bad weather. This east-coast road is the only option for motorists.

At Sligachan, an old hotel huddles alone under the mountains. It has been much modernised and extended in recent years, but its proudest boast is timeless – a view of the Cuillin that ranks among the most famous mountain panoramas in the world. It was at the Sligachan Hotel, too, that the pioneers of mountaineering celebrated their deeds and drowned their sorrows and commiserated about the weather, for the Cuillin in foul weather achieve a particularly rarefied form of purgatory. Norman Collie, Charles Pilkington, and the Skye man John Mackenzie wrote mountaineering history here. Like Nicolson, they were rewarded by having mountains named after them – Sgurr Thormaid, Sgurr Thearlaich and Sgurr Mhic Choinnich.

Sligachan was also a cattle market in its day, and in the 19th century crowds of several thousand were commonplace. (It should be remembered that in the mid 19th century, Skye's population was over 20,000.) Skye ponies were also sold at these markets, and vanished from the island to spend the rest of their lives labouring in the coal mines of the south, another particularly rarefied form of purgatory.

Sligachan has the feel of an island fulcrum. If there had been nothing more to Skye than Sleat and the Cuillin it would have been island enough for most people. But at Sligachan the road divides and opens up the four northern wings of Skye – Minginish, Duirinish, Waternish and Trotternish – wings that hover around a huge swath of high moorland. Now the land is utterly different. If there are summits they are flat-topped and wide. Inland the island is peat-deep and prosaic and thickened with unappetising conifer forests. But wherever the sea bites deep, and all along every outer shoreline, the land is energised, the light startles, history's spoor is everywhere, wildlife is varied and conspicuous, and you catch yourself forever looking over your shoulder to see if the Cuillin's latest re-invention of themselves is as staggering as the last one. Yes it is. It always is.

Loch Bracadale, 'a wide and deep bite of sea into the island's western flank...jewelled by its landmark lighthouse...'.

Sgurr nan Gillean, the Peak of the Young Men, dominates the northern profile of the Cuillin seen from the high moorland above Sligachan.

Talisker is not a drink, it is an interior explosion, distilled central heating; it depth-charges the parts, bangs doors and slams windows.

Derek Cooper, *Hebridean Connection.*

Topographically, Minginish is less 'wing' than the others. Some maps spill the word inland enough to embrace the Black Cuillin, but others settle for the wedge of low hills between Loch Brittle in the south and Loch Harport in the north. It is a place chiefly distinguished for being the birthplace of a malt whisky called Talisker. A tour of the distillery at Carbost is almost a religious experience for afficionados, something of the air of pilgrimage hovers around many a visitor. It is an acquired taste to be sure, with elements of peat and seaweed comingling on the drinker's palate, but once acquired, few drinkers are satisfied with anything else. Whether you succumb or are repelled, it is a remarkable whisky, distilled with a reverential approach to tradition, a Cuillin among whiskies, or a chief perhaps.

There are two more Taliskers, the Talisker River which leads a short and uneventful life until it reaches the sea, where it sweetens the oceanic salt of Talisker Bay, and Talisker Bay is as potent a distillation of the Skye coast as you will encounter.

Beyond Minginish is Loch Bracadale, another Skye arena famed for sunsets, a wide and deep bite of sea into the island's western

Neist Point lighthouse, the most westerly point of the island with a wide view of the Western Isles, and a grandstand for watching passing whales.

flank, and flecked by flattened-out islands and skerries and jewelled by its landmark lighthouse. And beyond Bracadale lies Duirinish.

Duirinish is westmost Skye, and the westmost tip of the westmost wing is symbolically extravagant. Neist Point is famous for a lighthouse at the end of the longest concrete path on Skye, but you are more likely to take away images of the 1000 ft cliffs of Waterstein Head, of the miles-wide sprawl of ocean and far islands (the smoky shapes of the Western Isles), and if you are lucky or patient or both, of passing whales. There is also a particularly spectacular example of that speciality of the Skye coast, the waterfall that falls straight into the sea. And in an onshore wind, the waterfall that is blown backwards as it tries to leave the island. There are no dull sensations where the westmost wingtip dips into the Atlantic.

So you have seen the mountains and the shores, the eagles, otters and the deer, you have tasted the human history and the whisky. You are now ready for the classical music. A second Borreraig near the north end of Duirinish has a more enchanting claim to fame than the wrecked Clearances village beyond the far shadow of the Cuillin. In the heyday of Clan society, the chiefs had a retinue of hereditary office-bearers, none

prouder than the hereditary piper. Pre-eminent among all pipers were the MacCrimmons of Borreraig on Loch Dunvegan, hereditary pipers to the chiefs of MacLeod. Borreraig was home to the MacCrimmons' piping college, and players from all over Scotland and Ireland came to study, lured by the beauty of the MacCrimmons' compositions and their skill as teachers. Let Seton Gordon explain the music and the MacCrimmons' mastery of it:

'It was perhaps in the seventeenth century that the most renowned MacCrimmon composers lived. At this time *ceòl mór* alone was played by the great pipers. *Ceòl mór*, or "big music", is the classical music of the Highland pipe. Each composition of *ceòl mór* is now known as a *piobaireachd* (pibroch). A *piobaireachd* is built upon a theme or *urlar*. After the *urlar* has been played,

The Vikings knew Loch Bracadale as Vestrafjord, Fiord of the West. Sunsets from its shores are among the most unforgettable of all Skye's spectacles.

19

The twin plateau-topped hills of MacLeod's Tables, seen here from near Harlosh, dominate the landscape around Dunvegan. The steep ascent is rewarded with fine views of the surrounding area.

one variation follows another, and the composition usually ends with the fast and difficult movements known as *crunluadh* and *crunluadh amach...*

'In the days of the MacCrimmons it is doubtful whether there was staff notation in pipe music, all the compositions of *ceòl mór* were handed down by a "word" notation called *canntaireachd*, which was sung by the old masters as they taught their pupils...each pupil had to memorise one hundred and ninety-five testing compositions of *ceòl mór* and be a master of theory and composition before he was held to have honourably finished his music course. Little wonder that there was a saying that it took seven generations of pipers to make a master player...'

Borreraig still has a piping school, and a piping museum, and the name of MacCrimmon is still revered on the lips of every serious piper the world over.

The history of Skye is often portrayed as one long conflict between its two great clans, the MacDonalds and the MacLeods, and certainly they spent a great deal of energy knocking lumps out of each other, countering outrage with greater outrage. Today's relationship is less fractious, and mostly settles for pointed jokes. Much as the MacDonalds like to trumpet the Clan Donald Lands around Armadale, they have nothing quite like the MacLeod seat of Dunvegan Castle.

You could not call Dunvegan Castle pretty, the pretensions of the 19th century have seen to that, but it likes to lay claim to being the oldest Scottish castle still standing. One tradition suggests Viking origins in the ninth century, but its known antiquity points to a 15th-century keep surrounded by water. Access from the land was a new invention when Boswell and Johnson visited in 1773. The sea gate remains, to be pondered over.

Among the castle's many treasures and relics is the mysterious Fairy Flag, the origins of which are gilded by an impressive array of contradictory legends. The most durable of these says that it may be waved three times when Clan MacLeod is in trouble. Twice it has been waved in battle, and twice the MacLeods prevailed. Now it reposes in a glass case, in readiness for a third waving. Whatever the truth of it, the Fairy Flag is a remarkable talisman for MacLeods everywhere.

The MacLeod seat of Dunvegan Castle, home of the mysterious Fairy Flag, of which a former chief once told a museum expert: 'You believe it to be a relic of the Crusades; I know it was given to my ancestors by the fairies.'

Waternish, a northern 'wing' of Skye with a reputation for unexplained mysteries and bloody legends.

Waternish is a string of road between the crest of a long hill and the sea, beginning with Fairy Bridge and ending with a ruined church famed for a massacre and as the last resting place of an infamous madwoman.

Jim Crumley, *The Heart of Skye*

Waternish, the third of Skye's northern wings, begins at Fairy Bridge, which may or may not have been where a particular fairy, who may or may not have been the wife of the MacLeod of the day, handed the MacLeod the Fairy Flag before leaving him forever to return to her Fairy world. The bridge itself is bypassed, but it has mysterious properties of its own. Horses have been known to refuse to cross, and all manner of otherwise rational islanders wave as they pass, to appease whatever it is about the bridge that needs appeasing. It is easy to scoff, as easy as it is difficult to attune to older eras when the unexplainable was still a stitch in the weave of everyday life and regarded fearfully. The mysterious goings-on at Fairy Bridge (unexplained murders, presences that discouraged travellers) ensured that Waternish was regarded by islanders as a place apart.

Blood is the common characteristic of Waternish legends and known historical events. The grimmest of these was the massacre at Trumpan Church in 1578, grim even by the standards of clan feuds. This is the massacre that MacDonalds like to be reminded of least when they bemoan their kinsmen's fate at the

Massacre of Glencoe.

What they did was, as usual, motivated by vengeance, in this case for the murder of 200 MacDonalds by MacLeods (also as usual), in a cave on Eigg. At Trumpan they set fire to the thatched church during a Sabbath service and those who escaped the flames died unarmed on MacDonald swords. An old woman squeezed through a window and raised the alarm, and sentries at Dunvegan Castle eventually saw the flames.

Ardmore Point, Waternish. Nearby is Trumpan Church, infamous setting for one of the most wretched of all battles between the MacLeods and the MacDonalds.

The MacDonalds were a select fighting force, the MacLeods a hastily gathered rabble, but...the Fairy Flag was waved! The subsequent battle slaughtered the MacDonalds on the shore, and their bodies were dumped in the shadow of a dyke which was then toppled over them. The battle, with commendable Gaelic irony, is known as the Battle of the Spoiling of the Dyke. It is commemorated, of course, by an exquisite MacCrimmon *piobaireachd*. Trumpan, far out on its headland, is an unchancy place still, where you can feel the chill on the warmest day.

Flora MacDonald's grave at Kilmuir near Uig in Trotternish. Her heroic part in the flight of Bonnie Prince Charlie was immortalised in 'The Skye Boat Song'.

The name of Flora MacDonald will be remembered always in Trotternish; her memorial stands in the small burying-ground at Kilmuir.

Seton Gordon, *The Charm of Skye.*

The fourth of Skye's great wings is Trotternish, a landscape of many astonishments, a symphony wrought in rock. It begins calmly enough if you board it discreetly by its Loch Snizort shore. From the west coast of the wing, you see only a hunchbacked landscape with occasional dark hints of the formidable face that stares eastward beyond the skyline, twists of dark rock that hint at hidden abysses. Uig is a village strung out along a cliff, and with deep enough water to accommodate the ferry to Harris. Kilmuir lies above and beyond a clutch of climbing hairpins, a village forever aching with loss. Flora MacDonald lies here, the heroine of Bonnie Prince Charlie's flight after Culloden. Her bold and colourful life is still wedded to that fateful acquaintance with the Prince, and more than 250 years after Culloden and all that, the Scottish throne is as empty and Stewart-less as it was when he fled his lost cause.

In a kind of supreme gesture of mockery, the MacLeod stronghold of Dunvegan displays Flora MacDonald's stays among its relics, without ever bothering to explain why.

Duntulm Castle is another MacDonald ruin. Its origins appear to be largely 15th century, and sometime between the middle of the 16th and the early 17th century, the MacDonalds vacated

Dunscaith on the Sleat coast and made Duntulm their seat, doubtless to fend off more aggression from the MacLeods. Derek Cooper notes in his book *Skye*:

'...the earliest mention of it occurs in the Description of the Isles appended to Skene's *Celtic Scotland* published in the 1580s: "Thair was an castell in Troutterness callit Duncolmend quhair of the wallis standis yet." They standeth still but largely through luck – a nineteenth century tenant of the farm of Duntulm had large portions of the castle blown up with gunpowder to get stones for a wall he was building...'

You don't suppose the farmer was a MacLeod? What survives is now being painstakingly restored, a relic on a tartan-patterned rock with the sea on three sides, staring one-eyed at the high hills of Harris. And if you look over your shoulder, you see the first swoops and piled contours of that geological phenomenon known as the Trotternish Ridge. There will be no let-up now. The symphony is getting into its stride.

The peaks of Sgurr Mor and Meall na Suiramach rear hugely above the wide moorland shelf of Skye's northeastern corner, and as you begin to travel south, Trotternish unveils the improbable architecture of the Quiraing. Locked away from the outside world

The wide bay of Lub Score at the north end of Trotternish with the ruinous MacDonald stronghold of Duntulm Castle on its headland. The writer Seton Gordon lived nearby.

One of the surprises of northern Skye is the panorama of the Western Isles. Lewis and Harris across the Minch look particularly close. The viewpoint here is Bioda Buidhe on the Trotternish Ridge.

behind pinnacles and buttresses and gullies and cliffs and every other imaginable and unimaginable configuration of broken rock is an isolated green lawn on top of one more lump of rock. The Table is unlike anything else in Skye or Scotland, and to walk its sward among the ricocheting vocables of raven and wren is to belong briefly to an indefinable realm which is not of our time. The hill road that crosses Trotternish between Uig and Staffin offers barely believable sightlines into the rock's unearthliness.

For most of the next 20 miles, the Trotternish Ridge's shattered eastern flank deals in huge gestures. It is largely the work of Ice Age vandalism on volcanic upheavals. The result is a massive landslip which still slips now, a snail's pace wreckage, nature defiling itself.

Even below the road, there are rock marvels, grace notes to the main symphony. The shore at Staffin beneath organ-pipe

The improbable rock architecture of the Quiraing.
The astounding green sward of the Table lies hidden behind
the highest buttresses and pinnacles.

cliffs is a layer of basalt pavement, like Staffa but with all the columns sawn off. It is not so much a shore as an edge, hard-topped and hard-bitten, a bizarre rock-platform wedged between butterflies and gannets, and a good place to recognise that the rock world of Trotternish is still on the move, still locked into an eternal conflict with itself, a collision of forces beyond our comprehension, the MacLeods and MacDonalds of geology.

The nearby Kilt Rocks have hardly suffered at all from a slight touristification. They remain cliff faces to marvel at, and with Loch Lealt behind, the sea in front, the mainland mountains strewn across the eastern horizon, and all manner of birdlife cruising between cliffs and seas, it is a place to while away captivated hours.

The Trotternish Ridge reaches a giddy conclusion at the Storr, where famed pinnacles strut the skyline, and just when you have consigned all that to your rear-view mirror, the Cuillin are gathering beyond Portree and you simply don't know where to look next.

It is no meagre thing, a journey among the primary feathers of the Winged Isle.

Staffin Bay seen from Bioda Buidhe on the Trotternish Ridge above the old road that crosses Trotternish from Uig to Staffin.

Arguably the most famous of all Skye profiles outwith the Cuillin – the Storr. The skyline pinnacle is the 160 ft Old Man of Storr, first climbed in 1955 by Don Whillans.

Portree, Skye's capital, is Port an Righ in Gaelic, the King's Harbour, named after the visit of James V in 1540. In recent years it has grown uphill from its wonderfully sheltered harbour.

'So the "eagle of the sunlit eye", as it is known in Gaelic, has joined the tourist business...'

Portree is a handsome capital, and for a Hebridean town, growing at a remarkable pace. It was named for James V who made a famous visit in 1540 and anchored in what is now the harbour, where sundry chieftains had gathered to pay their respects. Its name was changed more or less overnight to Port an Righ, the King's Harbour. But for long enough, it was little more than an inn and a sheltered anchorage, and 200 years ago it barely existed. The town was a MacDonald enterprise and grew at the hands of several chiefs, hence the presence of names like Somerled Square (Somerled, Lord of the Isles, founder of Clan Donald), Wentworth Street (named after the son of the 17th chief) and Bosville Terrace (a once common name among the Sleat MacDonalds).

The site is a remarkable one, and the restricted access to the harbour from the land has kept the worst excesses of commercial enterprise away from the waterfront. The seaward view is essentially a wild one, and the reintroduction of the white-tailed eagle to the islands has borne strange fruit here. With the entire western seaboard of Scotland at its disposal, the bird has chosen a cliff near Portree for one of its nesting sites, and boat trips out from Portree frequently produce sightings of its spectacular fishing technique.

At Portree's newest visitor centre, the Aros Experience, you can watch live pictures transmitted from a remote camera at the eyrie. So the 'eagle of the sunlit eye', as it is known in Gaelic, has joined the tourist business, one more grace note in the rock symphony that is Trotternish.

South of Portree, your eye is drawn inexorably to the growing proximity of the Cuillin. Wherever you have travelled in Skye, you have grown accustomed to their face, forever cropping up, forever changing shape and shade, forever unchanging. Above Sligachan, they blot out the known world, an unfurling of mountain shapes to satisfy the hungriest of eyes. With a light cloak of late spring snow about their summits and shoulders 'they rise like the hills of a land of dreams'. It should end, as it begins, with the Cuillin.

The Cuillin from Portree. Wherever you travel on Skye, the mountains have an endearing habit of cropping up unexpectedly, and unmistakably, on the skyline.

Rubha Hunish

Duntulm Castle (ruin)
Duntulm

Museum of Island Life
Flora MacDonald's
Grave & Memorial
Whitewave Outdoor Centre

To Tarbert
To Lochmaddy

Kilmuir
Linicro
Quiraing
Brogaig
Staffin

Prince Charles' Point

Uig
Uig Bay

Fairy Glen
Beinn Edra 611

Mealt Falls & Kilt Rock
Ellishadder

Lealt Falls

TROTTERNISH

Waternish Point

Waternish
Trumpan
Ardmore Point
Geary
Gillen
Stein
Lusta
Claigan
Greshornish
Kildonan
Kingsburgh

Loch Snizort

The Storr 719
Old Man of Storr

Rigg

Dunvegan Head
Piping Centre & Museum
Coral Beach

Loch Dunvegan
Borreraig
Giant Macaskill Museum
Milovaig
Toy Museum
Glendale
Colbost
Colbost Croft Museum
Neist Point
Ramasaig

Dunvegan Castle & Gardens
Fairy Br.
Dunvegan

Treaslane
Bernisdale
Edinbane
Skeabost
Borve

Kensaleyre

RONA

Sound of Raasay

Inner Sound

Brochel Castle (ruin)
Brochel
An Tuirean Arts Centre
Aros Experience

Torvaig

Ben Aketil 265
Rosgill
Ben Idrigill 341

DUIRINISH
"469
Orbost "488
Harlosh
MacLeod's Tables

Glen Ose Beinn na Cloiche 234
PORTREE
417 Beinn na Greine

Balgown

Raasay Outdoor Centre
Raasay Ho.

RAASAY

Sea of the Hebrides

Idrigill Point
Wiay
Port na Long
Fiskavaig
Rubha nan Clach

Loch Bracadale
Roineval 439
Glen Varragill
Ben Lee 444

The Braes

Bracadale
BB85
Loch Harport

Crowlin Islands
SCALPAY

Longay
Rubha na h-Uamha

Talisker
Talisker Bay
Carbost
Talisker Distillery
Drynoch
Sligachan
MINGINISH
Sg rr nan Gillean 965

773 Glamaig
Sconser
Marsco 736

Loch Ainort
Luib
Pabay

Serpentarium Environmental Centre

Kyle of Lochalsh

Glenbrittle
Sg rr Alasdair 1009
Cuillin Hills
Loch Coruisk
Blaven 927
Beinn na Caillich 732
Torrin

Broadford
Broadford Bay
Bright Water Visitor Centre
Kyleakin
Skulamus
Kylerea

Loch Brittle
Kirkibost
Loch Slappin
B8083
Clearance Village - Boreraig
Heast
Ben Aslak 605
Otter Haven

Rubh' an D nain
Loch Scavaig
Elgol
Loch Eishort
Ord
St. Comgan's Chapel (ruin)
Drumfearn
Glen Arroch

SOAY
Soay Sound

Dunscaith Castle (ruin)
Tokavaig
Isleornsay

Tarskavaig Point
Tarskavaig
Teangue
Knock Castle (ruin)

STRATHAIRD

Armadale Castle (part ruin) & Gardens
Museum of the Isles

Ardvasar
Armadale

CANNA
Sanday
Kilmory
RUM
Kinloch

Sound of Canna

To Eigg & Mallaig

Point of Sleat
Aird of Sleat
Ard Thurinish
Airor
KNOYDART

To Mallaig

© Wendy Price Cartographic Services 2005
Information used in the creation of this map came from the Royal Commission on the Ancient and Historical Monuments of Scotland and Peter Wright.

Trunk road
A road
B road
Minor road
Single track roads
Rail
Vehicle ferry
Passenger ferry

Castle
Garden
Golf course
Museum / visitor centre
Natural feature
Other place of interest
Boat trip
Tourist information (all year / seasonal)

0   5   10 km
0   5   10 miles

The Little Minch
Ascrib Islands

Loch Gairloch
Gairloch
Badachro
FLOWERDALE
Talladale
Loch Maree

Red Point
Redpoint
Rubha na Fearn
Lower Diabaig
Beinn Alligin 985
Fearnmore
TORRIDON
Liathach 1054
Upper Loch Torridon
"Cuaig
Torridon
Shieldaig
Beinn Damh 900
Loch Damh

APPLECROSS
Beinn Bh n 895
Applecross
Coulac

Toscaig
Kishorn
Lochcarron
Loch Kishorn
Loch Carron
Achmore

Plockton
Balmacara
Dornie
Totaig
Inverinate
Loch Long
Loch Duich
Ratagan
Shiel Bridge
Ben Sgriol 974
Arnisdale

Loch Alsh
Glenelg
Beinn na Seamraig
Loch Hourn
Ladhar Bheinn 1019
Luinne Bheinn 940
Inverie
Kinloch Hourn
Druim Fada 709
The Saddle 1011
Ben Sgriol 974
Sea of the Hebrides